Living Today for God

Living Today for God

by ROGER SCHUTZ, PRIOR OF TAIZE

translated by
Stephen McNierney
and Louis Evrard

HELICON PRESS

BALTIMORE MARYLAND

Introductory Letter

by Richard Cardinal Cushing

TWENTY-TWO years ago Roger Schutz, a Calvinist student of theology, formed a group of Protestants into an organization devoted to work, study, and prayer. He called it the Great Community and it was the beginning of what is now a monastic community in Taizé, France, which runs a children's refuge, organizes retreats and tries to further ecumenical relations.

In an attempt to advance the spirit of unity that motivated Roger Schutz, Helicon Press here publishes his valuable work under the title *Living Today for God*. Cardinal Cushing, who saw Schutz's manuscript, wrote the following letter:

Dear Father Prior:

I have read with great interest the English translation of your timely book, and have been deeply moved by the timeless spirituality which is reflected in its meditative pages.

The rule of your young community of Taizé—echoing in those pages—is most interesting indeed; it is the grace-full expression of a Christlike life. But that which I find most impressive is your application to our modern world of the evangelical counsels of poverty, chastity and obedience. How well do you see the problems and evils in our age which have come from worldliness, technology and disastrous dividedness! How wisely do you see that the remedy for those ills is the unity of Christendom! How prophetically do you propose the evangelical counsels as the means to this unity!

The generous spirit of poverty, the fertile activity of chaste love, the subjection to authority—these are the marks of the true followers of our Lord Jesus Christ, and, as you apply and present them to our modern world, they are the challenge which we modern Christians must offer the world. The more we imitate Our Lord on following these divine counsels, the closer we come to His Merciful and understanding Heart; and the closer we come to His Heart, the more we appreciate and the nearer we approach the perfect unity He prayed for and desires in His people, the Church.

I know that your book will find many interested readers in this country and—more importantly—I know and pray that many Americans will be deeply moved as I have been by your spirit, your words and the challenge you offer us. May God prosper its aims.

I am deeply grateful for the opportunity of reading your manuscript and I wish you and your work every blessing.

Sincerely in the Lord,
RICHARD CARDINAL CUSHING
Archbishop of Boston

Contents

Preface

by Henri Daniel-Rops

WHEN the day comes that it is possible to tell the whole story of these times, it will be necessary to recall all those brotherly communications, all those points of contact which are presently being built up between Christians of different confessions since the announcement, freighted with hope, of the Ecumenical Council. It will be an admirable, a moving story. We will be able to measure the signal importance of Pope John XXIII's gesture, by which he ordered reopened the doors of the Assembly which had been closed since 1870, and accompanied his decision with words very well suited to touch the hearts of the separated brethren. Whatever the concrete and tangible results of the Council, a new climate will be established and ties restored which only yesterday one would not have dared hope to renew. It is an important event of our day, one which revives confidence in a future that seems

terribly somber. In this story of the resumption of
fraternal ties there is a group of men in the fore-
front, and already associated with it, whom Catholics
must take into account in the light of charity and of
hope. One name denotes them: Taizé.

Taizé? Not far from Cluny, it is a little village
like many another in Burgundy. Roofs of red tile;
a very simple belfry surrounded with greenery. The
peasant one stops for directions indicates a little
slope, and at the top there stand high walls with a
portal. A motif of wrought iron crowns it, obviously
inspired by the frescoes of the catacombs of Cal-
lixtus: the mystic fish, the *ichthus*, repeated twice,
and encircled by the words *Communauté Taizé*.
Listen! A bell sounds, regular, conventual. The
echo of a chanted psalm reverberates. And, if one
waits until the office is finished, he will see file out
in Indian fashion—as at Solesmes or at Citeaux—
men vested in long white albs. To what order do
they belong, these "monks of Taizé," as the peasants
of the canton say? To none. They are Protestant.

In 1940, when France had just collapsed in defeat
and lay prostrate, a young man came to settle at
Taizé. He had delicate features, a manner at once
pensive and smiling. His name was Roger Schutz,
and from all appearances he came from afar.

He was a Swiss student born into a Protestant
family of solid Christian convictions. But a need for

the Absolute burgeoned in him which was not
satisfied by the life of a staunch member of a
reformed church in Geneva. "I was not truly a
Christian then . . ." he felt the need to say later.
A painful, quivering shaft fixed itself in him: how
was it that the best Protestants and the best Catholics, even those whose charity could not be doubted,
were so bitterly acrimonious as soon as the subject
of the other confession came up? Was it not fitting
that God should give an answer to this soul who
sought to understand?

Reading by chance a book on Port Royal—the
early Port Royal, before pride displaced purity of
intent—Roger Schutz had been moved by the expres-
sions of Mère Angelique and the Arnaulds, which
truly are quite poignant. A first step had been taken.
Another followed it when the encounter with Blaise
Pascal led the young Protestant from Geneva to
explore the undeniable truth of the celebrated wager.
From that moment, but still only half-consciously,
he made a resolution to stake his life as Pascal had
advised him, and he surrendered to that call of Grace
which Mère Angelique had made him understand.
Perhaps Roger Schutz believed that he was still the
faithful student of the Faculty of Theology of
Lausanne that he appeared to be to his associates,
but he was *in via*.

It was actually at this Protestant Faculty of Theology that a final vista was opened up to him by an invisible hand. He had chosen as the subject for a thesis the experience of St. Benedict, patriarch of monks and the real legislator for monasticism in the West. On studying the *Rule of Monks*, that masterpiece of organization and psychology, he wondered why, ever since the Reformation had shaken the Church and ruptured it so grievously, Protestants no longer had the custom—perhaps not even the right —of grouping themselves into communities of prayer like that of Monte Cassino. Why were there not Protestant cenobites just as there are Catholic monks, and Orthodox monks, and Ethiopian monks, to mention no more? This idea would have seemed foolish to a less generous and less daring spirit than Roger Schutz. To him, it seemed to offer the solution to his problems: he embraced it.

And that is why, in 1940, the young Genevan student bought a large empty house at Taizé, in Burgundy. At first he lived there alone, for two years. He was obliged to leave in 1942 and to return to Switzerland, as the Gestapo was a little too suspicious—justifiably, for the Jews and the resistance were using Taizé as a relay station—but Roger Schutz returned there as soon as he could, when Burgundy had been liberated. And this time he was no longer alone. Max Thurian, Pierre Souvairan and Daniel de Montmolin accompanied the founder. The

Great Community—great in its intentions rather than in the number of its members—was born. Nevertheless this number began to grow quickly. Let us pass over fifteen years. Today forty religious and ten novices are living at Taizé, not to mention the brothers—a dozen—who have been sent elsewhere, as we shall see. The rule of St. Benedict has served as a framework for all who have been accepted, and the members of the community take a vow to follow it after two years of novitiate. It imposes a triple obligation, the same as with Catholic monks: celibacy, obedience to one authority, community of goods.

Under the direction of a head recognized by all, the Prior (who is, of course, Roger Schutz), the brothers of Taizé lead the regulated existence of true religious. Three times a day—at seven o'clock in the morning, at noon, and in the evening—they come together in chapel for a meditative reading of the Psalms, prayers, and chant in common. Naturally, they also take their meals in common. The work which fills their days is varied. A school has been founded where fifteen children are being brought up whose parents were victims of the post war "purification," for at Taizé charity ignores political differences. There is a ceramics workshop, and also a printing office. Several fields are under cultivation. And for the rest, one leaves it to Providence . . .

The nature of the spirituality of the monks of Taizé is revealed in a priceless book, which bears an admirable title: *Living Today for God.* It is not without significance that it was first published by a Catholic house, the *Club du Livre Chrétien.* In writing it, Roger Schutz has been concerned to make clear, both for those Catholics and for those Protestants who are narrow of spirit and therefore might be scandalized, the true reason for his venture which is so paradoxical in appearance. For him, there is only one scandal: the scandal of disunited Christians, our disobedience to the supreme command of the Master: "That all be One!" It is only the ecumenical perspective, in which separated brethren ought to meet each other again in the charity of Christ, that offers a fitting appreciation of this effort and this thought. However Roger Schutz analyzes "the dominant forces of the modern world," however he responds to the terrible threats that he sees, by an appeal to the "dominant values of the interior life," his book is written with one single intention: that all Christians, whatever the confession they belong to, may find there nourishment for the soul. The result is so magnificent that *L'Osservatore Romano* has rendered him homage. "We could say nothing that is at the same time more evangelical, wiser, and more human," said a prince of the Church, Cardinal Gerlier.

"It is impossible," François Mauriac says some-
where, "to write words which have a Christian ring
without strangers being drawn to them. . . . Certain
words have kept all their power over a hungry humanity." Better than so many other men, Roger
Schutz knows this power is that of Christ alone and
his message, and it is this power that explains the
radiance of Taizé. At the same time the little groups
of spiritual commandos, the brothers, have been sent
to Marseilles as dock workers, to Algiers as brick-
layers among the Moslems, to Abidjan and even to
the United States. And a Protestant community for
women has just been established, as the properly
ecumenical activity of Taizé expands.

Two of the great Catholic spirits of our day have
been closely associated with the effort of Roger
Schutz: the Abbé Couturier who gave his life, even
to his last breath, to the cause of reconciling the
churches; and Mgr. Chevrot, the celebrated curé and
member of the Institute. The Bishop of Autun, in
whose diocese Taizé is located, does not hide the
sympathy which he feels for this unique endeavor.

Such is the experience of Taizé—unique, incomparable, and one which a Catholic would not know
how to consider without warmth. As for those—of
one or another confession—who would see there
some sort of suspect beginnings of proselytism, of
confusionism, of syncretism, let them consider this

little story. There was a lad, somewhat misguided, who came to Roger Schutz to confide that he wished to abandon the Catholic faith and leave a group not far from there where the priests are doing fine apostolic work. It was the Prior of Taizé who brought him home to his native fold . . .

Foreword

THE purpose of this book is to aid reflection on the world and the Church of today. It has been written at Taizé, a community that aims at being— at the same time—in the world and in the heart of the Church (with a full awareness of the tragedy of a divided Christianity), and therefore the contents of this small volume may appeal as having a certain authenticity.

A Protestant, however, may well ask: "What can a community like Taizé reveal about unity to us, since it does not mirror what exists in our Churches?" True indeed, how could it mirror the Reformed Churches, as it is still the only monastic community for men that has arisen so far within those Churches? But although it has had so far a unique vocation within them, this is far from preventing it from being a part of them, and leads it to seek precisely within them the path towards visible unity among Christians.

Many Protestants agree, of course, on the need for ever more ardent prayer that we be granted unity, and admittedly prayer is the chief way and is open to all. But if such prayer does not lead to action, does it not remain an escape from a painful reality and its costly demands upon us?

Yet never does prayer fail to bring about an expansion of Christian charity. We at Taizé have recognized this most vividly in the last few years. Men once far from us have become brothers in faith. Thanks to the same supernatural charity there have been laymen, priests, bishops, and cardinals who have been able to understand what we have to say to them even though by human standards we were widely separated from them in background and temperament. Through this charity they have come to appreciate what in Protestantism is most authentic, serious, and attentive to the truths of the Good News.

How wonderful it would be if within the Roman Church the number of men of such understanding would increase in our time.

If the barriers which once confronted us had not been surmounted by the friendship which Christ places in men by the Holy Spirit we would still be at the stage of those endless discussions which are forever breaking down over some rational difficulty. We would still be mired in sterile debate.

I cannot resist citing an excellent example of this irenical spirit. After reading the pages which follow, Cardinal Gerlier wrote to me: "Thank you for recalling to us once again the conformity with the Gospel and the value for our own day—these two are but one—of poverty, celibacy and obedience. But what I found most compelling in your work—others will perhaps have different impressions—is your treatment of contemplation, of the common possession of goods, of the exercise of authority in community, and of the common life in obedience and unity.

"In an epoch in which hundreds of millions of human beings suffer from hunger it is necessary to recall the value of choosing to hold in common the goods of this earth. Can anyone reread without emotion the words of St. John Chrysostom and St. Basil on this subject . . . ?

". . . Finally, at a time in which so many attempts are being made to achieve a true life in common, I think that all who are engaged in this effort will meditate with interest on the rules of Taizé. I know of nothing more in keeping with the Gospel, more wise, and at the same time more human.

"With all my heart I hope that these pages may teach your readers to confront the world more fully with their faithfulness to Christ, and to be ever more concerned with unity among themselves. No doubt we shall have to learn to wait—you deal well with the subject of patience—but we must also nourish a boundless hope based on the promise of God and on the prayer of his beloved Son."

In the same irenical spirit, Pastor Marc Boegner, president of the Protestant Federation of France, wrote to me:

"The proof of friendship and trust which you have shown me in asking me to read before its publication the work which will soon appear from the Press of Taizé has deeply touched me and I offer you my affectionate thanks.

". . . You will not be surprised that I found of particular interest everything in your work that touched directly or indirectly on the problem of the unity of the Church and on ecumenical activity. Your reflections are carried on in the context of the world of today and of the Church upon which her Lord has laid such fearful demands with regard to this world. These give rise to the awful tension which Christians of today, if they wish to be true followers of Christ, must accept as the very law of their life. You have received the grace to see clearly the only path on which you may remain: in this same tension, humbly and joyously faithful to your ecumenical vocation—the path of love.

". . . I bless you, then, for recalling to us that the royal road which will lead us over humanly insur-

mountable barriers to the visible manifestation of
the unity of the Body of Christ is the path of the love
which 'believes all things, hopes in all things, suffers
all things, and is never confounded.' "

ROGER SCHUTZ
Taizé

Dominant Characteristics
of Today's World

SINCE the fourth century there have been few historical periods as decisive as our own. Either modern Christianity will realize one of the first demands of the Gospel, the sense of the universal, or Christian churches will become inbred in the small areas of the world in which they are found today and become obstacles to the expansion of grace, "the source of salvation for all men."

This century thus confronts all Christians with an option of life or death. Today they are less than a billion, divided among numerous creeds and surrounded by a billion and a half non-Christians. What will they be when at the end of this century mankind will count four billion? Even today a still-divided Christianity faces an ideology of militant atheism which, for the first time in history, also makes a claim of universality.

But if Christianity even wants to manifest its desire to establish a community of all these millions, its first step must be to unite in an attempt to remove the first obstacle—to achieve, that is, an equitable distribution of the goods of this earth. We must face the fact that countries with a very high proportion of Christians possess greatly disproportionate wealth, while non-Christian countries are pinched for lack of material resources. At the midpoint in this century, for instance, the standard of living in the United States was thirty-five times as high as in India. Christians' response to this portentous disproportion may well determine the future of Christianity.

Besides removing that obstacle, at the same time we shall have to have a heart large enough, an imagination open enough, and a love warm enough to find a way to break through the denominational bonds that restrict us and, by rediscovering visible unity among Christians, to become capable of communicating our faith to the non-Christian world.

How can we achieve communion with this world and still remain within the Church, the Body of Christ? Ever striving to live profoundly rooted in the Church, how can we even meet members of the present-day non-Christian world in order to bring them our most precious possession, our love of Christ?

The answer is that every true relationship with

Christ leads us toward our neighbor. Yet a difficulty remains, for, paradoxically, established Christianity—particularly as it grows older—tends to remove us from our neighbor, at least in our dealings with certain categories of men.

Each time we return to the Gospel we should be renewed in our appreciation of the brotherhood of man. Yet our ancient Churches, encumbered by the weight of civilization, tend to monopolize a man, to enclose him in a world apart.

In addition, by a retrogressive tendency, we Church members too often turn toward the past and lose touch with our own day. This attitude, arising from motives which we sometimes will not admit, then leads us to build for ourselves a circle of like-minded companions in which it is pleasant to live together and thus little by little to organize ourselves into a sort of Christian ghetto. The extent of this isolation may not become apparent until one notices how impossible it has become for many Christian groups to establish any sort of communication with the unattached, unbelieving masses oriented towards the present.

Facing up to the fact that many of our neighbors have become detached from the Christian faith, we Christians must go out of our way to meet and come to know those neighbors. We must seek them where they are to be found—in the world; and this means the world of the present day. More than ever we must keep abreast of social, political, and economic conditions. We must know the world, over which Christ reigns but in which His sovereignty is today ignored. But knowing the world requires a willingness to accept facts in a disinterested and objective spirit; more than anyone else, the Christian must be capable of the detachment necessary to "dispassionalize" a situation. He must no longer be a man with interests limited to a ghetto of rigid judgments and one-sided opinions.

To orient ourselves in our de-Christianized milieu, we shall do well to consider at some length here several characteristics of the modern world which are among the dominant marks of our century:

The search for unity on the part of the masses
The growth of population
The acceleration of developments of all kinds
Hunger
The division of the world into two blocs
The desire to "live one's own life"

1. *Just when so many Christians are losing the sense of universality, the masses are seeking a worldwide unity*

Within a few decades, distance has lost its former scale. Ever more rapid means of transportation and communication have, in turn, accelerated the inter-penetration of the races. Even in the farthest outposts of civilization, radio links man to the rest of the world. All over the world so linked there is growing a kind of universal humanity with identical habits; one need think only of the success of the unimaginative western styles of dress among peoples who once knew the flowing garments of the East alone.

All across the world the men without Christ, the proletarian classes, are discovering their solidarity. This discovery is developing rapidly, and like all present-day developments is in fact moving at a pace which those accustomed to the rhythm of earlier decades find disconcerting. Christians, accustomed as they are to life in a stable, retrospective social group, often have great difficulty in detecting within this quickening tempo of world development the underlying drive toward unity in moral outlook and in living patterns. They lag behind. By this very fact, the Church is ignored. When she does make herself known, she is usually judged severely by the working class as an outmoded society, incapable of keeping up with the times.

Some Christians, similarly pained at the slow progress of their fellow believers and looking for progressive formulas, become so impatient as to dis-associate themselves from those who, like themselves, bear the name of Christ.

Indeed, the working classes are a reproach to us. Divided as we are into numerous creeds, we Christians cannot even bear witness among ourselves to the love of Christ. Meanwhile, the godless masses which surround us are striving toward brotherhood, often with a very lively sense of their common humanity. Today, unbelievers who seek to create this universal brotherhood bring to that effort a lucidity, a capacity for self-criticism, and sometimes a good will which contrast sharply with the attitude of the many Christians who spend their time spying on one another and live only to defend parochial aims.

This clouded atmosphere of self-congratulation and mutual distrust has caused many Christians to flee the Church in a desperate attempt to live without her in the midst of a world indifferent to many things for which Christians stand. The simple fact of this flight represents a judgment which weighs heavily on all of us. But the rupture between the churches and a world no longer part of them is serious for another reason: the leaven of unity mixed with the dough is no longer the Gospel.

We must understand the motives which prompt this striving towards brotherhood on the part of the working classes. We must try to accept in the depths of our beings the present state of the world as an indirect appeal to all Christians to fulfill a vocation, the catholicity of the Church. Finally, we must exert in the world an influence that is always valid, namely, the combining in our own persons of the world and the Church.

This only they can achieve who refuse to judge in advance the often excessive impulses of the working class, who are not afraid to get their hands dirty, and refuse to seek a personal salvation without any reference to the rest of mankind.

Embracing in one's self both Church and world can be done in a number of ways. Some will accept a life in the heart of the masses. Others will seek to know better and to make known the world over which Christ reigns. Still others will take the path of prayer, for in contemplation one can play an authentic part in the world often more valid than devoted social work or a philanthropic program carried on apart from the Church.

2. *World population is increasing at an unheard of rate*

At the beginning of this century, one half of the world was Christian. In the year 2000 perhaps only one-fourth will be.

A few figures: In 1900, after the great expansion of missionary activity, there were 800,000,000 Christions among a total population of 1,500,000,000— one Christian out of every two human beings. Today there is one Christian in every three, since the total population has grown to 2,600,000,000 without a really significant increase in the size of the Christian community. In the year 2000 the population will undoubtedly total more than 4,000,000,000. Will Christians then number only one in four?

This staggering growth of humanity manifests itself above all in the Far East, precisely in those areas where Christians represent only an insignificant part of the total population. Thus the Church finds itself in a changing position. The Christian communities are located chiefly among those peoples whose birth rate is lowest. The countries with the strongest population growth rates are those which are most violently opposed to everything which comes from the West, including the Church.

What will be the answer of Christians confronted with this increase in human population?

Scientific investigations to determine the precise character of this growth in population at any particular point on the globe, maps and statistics to chart current sociological phenomena, and the Church's missionary statistics rich in information are all very well. But if we were to content ourselves with an exclusively sociological appreciation of the facts we could very quickly become hypocrites, capable only of making pronouncements on the world situation and proposing general remedies for it. We would have stopped half way. The knowledge of the drama implied in today's population growth must impel us to encourage among men and women the vocation to bring about concrete solutions.

Once again, enlightened prayer is the best weapon available to all. By faithfully recommending to the Lord of the Church the hardships of this or that people we remain in contact with the drama of the life of men today. Prayer implies a willing awareness of everything which concerns the masses.

To pray for the increasing multitude who live in the world without God is already to lay the groundwork for missionary activity. Yet our response to duty will be entirely honest only if the Christian presence at the heart of the increasing populations is effectively a missionary one.

At the present time when we meet those who reject us or do not know who we are, we ourselves are divided, Christians opposing one another. How can men be effectively brought to believe that Christ is the One sent by God if they do not see Christians united in their faith and their testimony? The rapid growth of population may well be one of the factors which will spur Christianity toward visible unity.

It should be noted that the missionary impetus does not necessarily imply an evangelization in the traditional sense. When introduced under the protection of a colonizing western power, the Gospel has often been mixed with compromises of which it will have to be purified. Today the silent example of a discreet presence among non-Christians will sometimes be justified as tending to rehabilitate the white, Western, and therefore suspect Christian. We know that we are Christbearers, Christ's ambassadors. We can fulfill this role humbly by a life hidden in the heart of the masses of a missionary country, affording mute evidence that the Gospel is disinterested.

3. *The acceleration of developments of all kinds*

A few facts will suffice to recall the extent of this acceleration:

In agriculture, methods of cultivation remained the same from Roman times until the end of the nineteenth century. In fifty years the sickle has given way to the combine.

The evolution of transportation is even more staggering. The airways which encircle the globe unite a humanity once partitioned by geographical bounaries.

In the United States developments in industry, society, and living conditions have accelerated to such an extent that the man who wishes a history of the country must buy the edition of the current year, since profound changes no longer occur decade by decade but month by month. For example, social conditions for Negroes are quite different from what they were just a few years ago. Similar acceleration of change is to be seen in large areas in present-day Russia.

Fully organized cities, once the work of centuries, in the modern world spring up in a few years. The poorer populations flock to these wealthy centers. The cities, soon unable to absorb the surplus, leave the new arrivals to settle in sprawling shanty towns, cities of misery alongside centers of luxury.

At the dawn of the atomic era we can sense the significance for all continents of the transformations due tomorrow. Changes whose rhythm began to pick up in the last century will accelerate even more; even we ourselves, men of the twentieth century, can scarcely imagine what the next few years will bring.

4. *Hunger in the world is on the increase*

Those who once had enough now have still more. Those who once had next to nothing now have still less. Famine areas are also the areas of largest population growth. Current thought ascribes this coincidence to a physiological phenomenon: the absence of certain kinds of foods leads to an increase in the production of the hormones necessary for procreation. Thus underdeveloped peoples have the highest population growth, a fact which brings with it an ever more serious shortage in their food supply.

In Christian countries, on the other hand, the

goods of this world abound. How can we change
this situation so as to share our bread with the
hungry? Can we pray sincerely for those who have
nothing as long as we keep more than we need? We
must respond to an essential demand of the Gospel
by sharing our bread with the hungry. Christians of
the twentieth century will be judged in large measure
by the answer to this problem which they provide or
stimulate.

Today, those who are trying to awaken the Christian conscience in this matter are still scattered and
few in number. One of them, Josue de Castro, gave
up a position which humanly speaking was very
useful to society in order to grapple concretely with
this problem. His *Geopolitics of Hunger* has already
served to bring about a change in Christian circles.
There have also been the first timid attempts at
taking up a collection among Christians of one
denomination for the benefit of those of another,
until then in opposition. In such a way, through our
love and concern for the poor of Christ, we can
betoken our friendship and reconciliation.

5. *The world today is divided into two political
blocs, corresponding to two ideologies apparently in
contradiction*

In the midst of the tension between East and West
what should our attitude be? The Christian cannot

refuse to live in the midst of the tensions of this world, but he cannot allow himself to be carried away by the passions they engender. More than ever before he must be a man of peace, lest he become unable to live fully in the world without being of the world. If he holds his own heart at peace in the sight of God he will in turn help other men to give up the fear which leads to hatred and to war.

The Christian must recognize clearly the attraction which the world holds for him. He must realize that the power of the world to secularize is an awful one. In the West the world exerts this power through material conveniences which tend to act as tranquilizers and hence to quench our concern for our neighbor. When these labor-saving devices are no longer used as instruments with which to work, it would be better not to have them at all. In Eastern countries the power of secularization can exert the same force on Christians. The cult of the masses, the sense of working-class solidarity, the concern for the redistribution of wealth—all these things can divert our attention to an illusory paradise and cause us to forget the essence of the Gospel.

If the tension between East and West is maintained for long, we Christians will be under pressure to engage ourselves on one side or the other. At times the Christian will then have to declare himself a conscientious objector to his being made a member of a party. In order to live in the midst of today's tension we must insist more than ever on the one essential thing, the freedom of the Gospel, which is bound up with the freedom of a man to live according to that Gospel. This liberty must never be confused with any sort of natural liberalism. Engulfed as we are in today's turmoil between East and West, we must face up to events. Refusing to be influenced by passion, we must master ourselves so as to become men of God, that is, men of peace.

6. *The rising generation wants only to live its own life*

This generation insists on its right to its own existence. It wishes to give free play to the development of the human person. It distrusts history, the experiences of the past. It wants to live its personal experiences, and to live them now. It wants to be, to exist, to live, rather than to construct systems. Perhaps this sense of urgency comes from the sensation of living at the final hour, the one which precedes the end of an entire era if not the final annihilation of a civilization.

People often talk of "living their own lives." This attitude implies giving free rein to the senses. The climate is as though charged with sex, and this phenomenon is even more obvious in the countries of North America than in the older civilization of

Western Europe. On a busy street corner a billboard, a moving picture marquee, or a newsstand will be crying out for this realization of one's being. Songs exalting carnal love have never had so many lyricists and performers. In addition, the same song is spread by radio from Paris to Tokyo. Sometimes this frenetic need to live is further encouraged by half-digested theories of psychology and psychoanalysis.

In response to feverish reactions to the fear of annihilation tomorrow the Christian must face up to his responsibilities; he must remind himself that the Gospel itself contains a form of existentialism, a startling call to live in this very day which the Lord has made. The Christian loses his joy as soon as he worries about the morrow. There is a folly in the Gospel which contradicts man's need for security.

As for the desperate sexuality of our times, it would be easy for those of us who live in the climate of Western civilization to adopt a puritanical attitude and to try to place young Christians in bad faith with regard to the life of the senses. Such education, whatever its former effectiveness with unevolved mentalities, today runs the risk of achieving exactly the opposite result. Every trace of narrow-mindedness, every snap judgment serves only to separate us irrevocably from the younger generation. The only solution is to remain fully human. This we do when we know how to help our neighbor find himself moral values to which he will be able to conform without external coercion.

In any case, the way in which we conduct ourselves before the world will be more convincing than words. If we truly live the sign of contradiction presented to the world by the irrevocable fidelity of Christian spouses or by the chastity of the celibate who embraces his life as a response to the call of Christ, we can be sure that the seed planted in the earth will grow by night and by day.

Dominant Values of the
Interior Life

ANYONE who writes about the interior life of the Christian must emphasize at the outset that spiritual directives are relative to concrete situations. It is, therefore, one thing to read or write of them, and another thing to live by them.

But one licit generalization—and the first we must grasp—is that the whole person must be animated by the interior life: body, soul, and spirit. One cannot keep watch only over his thoughts or only over his body. Between the physical and the psychical there is such an intimate connection, such a complete reciprocity, that a disturbance in one leads to disturbance in the other.

Mind and body are one. The basis of self-discipline lies in holding both open, susceptible to the action of God. The aim is to maintain the creature in communion with the Creator. The only end, the rule of Jesus Christ over the whole person.

1. *Interior life and a rule of life*

Can interior discipline, then, consist in the sub-
jugation of matter to spirit, the death of sense and
of body? Should living be "the application of oneself to dying," according to the formula of Plato?

The matter-spirit dualism does not exist in the
Gospel. On the contrary, God is made flesh. He has
taken on a human body. He has dwelt among us.

The struggle of life is not a fight of the spirit of
man to conquer the body. It is the struggle of the
Spirit of God to captivate all of the capacities of a
man.

Christian asceticism, therefore, has nothing in
common with mere self-denial. It is never an end
in itself, but a means to respond to grace. Nevertheless, the exhortation to cut off the hand that
occasions the fall serves to remind us that Christian
asceticism is self-denial indeed, even requiring extreme measures in cases where all other remedies
fail; but we proportion the rigor to the need, in much
the same way as a doctor amputates only after all
other possibilities have been exhausted.

The response of man to grace, then, will be the
submission of his person to the action of the Spirit
of God. There is no need to tax one's brains to
decide upon privations to take upon oneself. Mas-
tering one's self is program enough. Instead of going
beyond what God asks of us it would be better to

perform with simplicity of heart the demands of the present day. Unconsciously our heart can prefer certain ideal requirements to those of the present situation. We are asked to walk patiently along the path traced for us by God, and yet, obsessed with self-denial, we refuse the abundance of gifts offered to us in order to turn back upon ourselves, to fix our attention on our own sins rather than on the incomprehensible forgivingness of God. We seek by ourselves the remedy to our hidden evil, even though God offers us the solution through the means of grace available in the Church.

In the advance toward self-mastery it is important to keep our eyes fixed, not on details, progress or regression, but on the goal: Christ Jesus. Otherwise we shall confuse the means with the end. We shall come to meditate more on man than on God, that is, to scourge ourselves for our sins rather than magnify God for his forgiveness.

Need we fear that interior discipline may lead us to form such mistaken attitudes as formalism or as the desire for perfection as a thing in itself? These dangers must be faced, but they need not paralyze us nor keep us rooted to one spot. The Christian is a man on a tightrope. Only God can maintain the equilibrium of the man who accepts the challenge of Christianity: running toward Christ.

Formalism and habit—each day they stifle a man

whose spiritual discipline is no longer enlivened by the love of Christ and neighbor. If it is a good thing to force yourself to pray at regular hours, this is for the love of the Lord and not for the sake of a law. Certainly the regularity of prayer will sometimes weigh heavily. Ours is a nature in revolt against its Lord. Only when we allow our love for Christ to grow cold do we run the risk of experiencing our rule of regular prayer and meditation as a new law unto itself.

Remember the counsel: we must be even more faithful during times of spiritual dryness than on those days in which faith leads us spontaneously to prayer and recollection. On such difficult days we must remind ourselves of the answers to prayer we have received previously and of the hours filled with the presence of God. The only defense against formalism and habit is precisely to remain faithful to one's rule of prayer, and in its application to strive always for fervor and adoration.

"The men who have accomplished most are those who have known how to direct their lives in strength and tranquillity, above all if they have been able to join this fidelity to a liveliness of spirit, a warmth of soul which does not always accompany this spirit of rule and method but which, when linked to them, makes a man capable of the most outstanding things" (A. Monod, *Les Adieux*).

In our interior life a rule will play the role of a teacher. Without a rule we risk forgetting our most noble resolutions. It is necessary also to summarize as far as possible a few words from the Gospels in a form which can be easily remembered.

Our rule should translate the thought of Christ into words which strike our mind most forcibly, the more personal the better. This is the adaptation of the Word of God to a particular situation. Deeply pondered, slowly elaborated, the fruit of a long development and usually forged in struggle, our rule, once discovered, must be obeyed. In this way it will become a powerful force in our inner life. By narrowing the field of alternatives it will allow us to build with resolution. It will give a unity to the inner life because it will lead us in a determined direction for the whole of our life.

What counts is not the number of guiding principles but the obedience in the present moment to a few directives which are sufficiently clear and succinct to be constantly remembered. We must have a rule which we have decided to follow to the end, one to which we return each time we realize that we have forgotten it. Such a rule will become easy to the extent that it is boldly practiced. He who is entirely patient, who does not seek to reap prematurely the fruits of his effort, who is willing to bide his time, will finally see the day on which he will do easily what once cost him vigorous effort. Unknown to him the rule will have been forming his interior being.

The aim of the rule is to create a profound unity for him who perseveres, who is no longer constantly re-examining his rule but always beginning anew to follow it. Christian life is nothing but a perpetual beginning anew, a return in grace each day and sometimes each hour to Him who, after each fall, grants His pardon so that all things may be made new.

On days of weariness we must continue our self-imposed discipline, sighing that we fulfill it without joy and without love. If it should become impossible to live up to it, we must abandon ourselves to Christ. When the inner flame seems extinguished it is still possible to wait in silence, remembering that "out of the barren soil a rose has bloomed."

2. *Interior life and contemplation*

A communication is established in the interior life between the Christian and Christ. This personal relationship, renewed by prayer, meditation, and communion of the Body and Blood of Christ, leads the Christian to grasp the presence of God in contemplation.

A Western mentality easily finds itself in spontaneous opposition to this type of communication. The juridical turn of mind which we have inherited through European Christianity from ancient Rome is a poor preparation for this highpoint of the interior life, contemplation. In the Eastern Churches, in contrast, this reality is still lived intensely in our day. Much less concerned about precise definitions of our knowledge of God, their mentality accords a much higher place to adoration.

We Western Christians easily remain dissatisfied as long as so much of the truth of the Gospels has not yet been grasped by reason. We force our faith to rationalize itself. By so doing we risk robbing the salt of its savor. In our desire to understand we can dry up a spring which was there to refresh the interior life.

Contemplation is sometimes defined quite negatively as the opposite of action. On these terms it would be a luxury reserved to those Christians who refuse to incarnate their faith among men. Yet history tells quite a different story. Some Christians have experienced the fullness of contemplation while remaining at the same time very much engaged in the life of men, overflowing with activity. St. Theresa of Avila engaged in commerce, discussed business, wrote, and at the same time lived intimately with God in the depths of her being. It is not for nothing that this woman has remained the classical example of the contemplative.

If we rid ourselves of our negative reactions to

contemplation, what may we understand by it? Nothing other than the disposition in which the being in its totality is seized by the reality of the love of God. When we grasp a natural truth with our intellect we are sometimes captivated by it, but only partly so. But we can be overcome entirely, to the very depths of our hearts, by supernatural truth, by the love of God. Love is here the touchstone. In intimate connection with the love of God, contemplation leads us to love of neighbor. John, the apostle of contemplation, warned himself against the hypocrisy of anyone who would profess with his lips to love God while at the same time hating his brother.

Contemplation molds our love of God. If it is authentic, this clinging with all one's being to Christ cannot help manifesting itself in our relationships with our neighbor. Conversely, the love which we bring to our fellow man places the seal of genuineness on our contemplation.

I have in mind two men, both of whom received the same vocation. One makes no progress. The other races along. He knows how to "reject useless burdens . . . and run . . . keeping his eyes on Jesus." Both men have the same desire to do what is demanded of them.

The one suffers constantly. He is hypersensitive to his neighbors' reactions. When he meets new people, he finds he cannot renew within himself the kind of compassion which allows one to accept others completely as they are. His soul is as though asleep.

The other receives the same injuries, yet he preserves through everything a joy that is rarely confounded. For the first, death is preferable to a life in God. For the second, the only thing of importance is a charity constantly enlivened by a contact with his neighbor.

This is a disturbing discovery. In the first case both compassion and the very simple sense of forgiveness are as though asleep. A life among men has become intolerable. In the case of the man who lives in the presence of Christ, the very difficulty of rubbing shoulders with his neighbor, far from presenting an obstacle, quickens his pace.

One thing is certain—all communication with God leads toward one's neighbor. The authentic sign of all interior life, of all relationship with Jesus Christ, is the discovery of one's neighbor. If our neighbor disappears from our dialogue with Christ, our love for God is founded upon a mythical divinity having no relationship with our humanity, rather than upon the Christ of the Gospel. The soul of man without God is devoured by love; the soul of the Christian smothers if its love for God excludes love for neighbor.

Contemplation allows one to grasp with love a truth of God. It is given to the simple of heart. In his interior life a Christian can be the bearer of only a very few essential truths. Once he has grasped them he must develop them. His Christian life passes through shadow and sunlight, from forgetfulness of the treasure confided to him to a sudden realization of its value.

Happy are the simple. Those who have the spirit of simplicity possess the kingdom. Theology, the science of God, the accumulation of knowledge—these things bring with them no extra privileges in the contemplation of the divine mystery. Rather they are often a distraction from it. As though in his justice, God grants a revelation of his presence to the humble, to the little ones of this world. The only thing to do is to "keep these things to ponder them in one's heart" and to live this presence of God discovered face to face.

Nothing perceptible marks those who are the object of such attention on the part of the Lord. Should all of these gifts display themselves, a primary position of the ego would still be suspect in this moment in which God is everything. There would then be an illusion of contemplation. Must not even those who fast and abstain anoint their hair and wash their face, so that their fast will be known to the Father alone and not to men? And we must be aware that in the visible phenomena of prayer one skirts the limit of the supernatural, near neighbor of the diabolical.

Contemplation remains a way open to every Christian. It is true that those for whom prayer is a thirst are rare. As a result, many believers become fatigued when confronted with the difficulties of talking with God. Some go for months and even years without being given the means to renew contact with God in prayer. Must one immediately begin talking of dryness and spiritual night? Certainly not, since this in itself might be a call to contemplation. Little by little there arises within us a silence, within which the values of this world take on their true importance. One thing only becomes necessary. Even a difficulty in expressing oneself in prayer can be a call, purified of all externals, to a communion with Christ.

Contemplation is adoration. Prayer leads us to dialogue. It intellectualizes situations by bringing them within the field of human understanding in order to present them to God. Meditation requires a search which is sometimes laborious, but in contemplation our regard is fixed upon one single truth to which we cling with all our being.

Since it engages the whole man, contemplation of the God of Jesus Christ cannot lead to quietism. On the contrary, it moves us to bold action and rules out

the possibility of lukewarmness. It commits us irrevocably to the race. He who runs will discern the
track, no matter how faintly. The man whose course
is directed by the vision of Christ knows where he is
going. Two rules for running are interdependent
and must always be observed: Forget that which lies
behind, forget progress or regression, and fix your
gaze attentively on Him who guides our faith.

The way in which we fasten our gaze upon the
invisible Christ determines the entire transformation
of our being. This transformation can be quite im-
perceptible to us and undoubtedly it is better that it
should be. Enough for us to know that night and day
the seed takes root and grows without our knowing
how.

We must run this race, then, and for this we must
fix our eyes on the God of the prophets and of
Christ, ever awaiting the day on which Christ Himself will turn his eyes toward us. Only those who
have come to know him are capable of overflowing
and compassionate love for their neighbor. Blessed
are the humble whose hearts are pure, for they shall
see God!

Living in the World

WE have described certain characteristics of the world today and pointed out in each instance the way in which our Christian life can achieve itself in the midst of the life of men. A few more brief indications might be useful.

1. *Simplifying our existence*

In the material order we must quietly and constantly be taking stock of the means we possess both for our work and for our life in general, with an eye toward getting rid of everything which is not essential and which might encumber us. Furniture, books, documents, clothes—possessions of all kinds can slowly and without our being aware of it weave about us a cloak of lead which paralyzes our movements.

On the intellectual level this simplification will lead us to accept our limitations. There is no need

to overtax our will; we need not be walking ency-
clopedias. Our part is to build on a human scale.
We can safely leave to the geniuses what is their
own. No one realizes how many minds are actually
disordered by the accumulated fatigue brought on
by efforts to attain an unreasonable level of knowledge. It would be well to remember the advice of
Sertillanges: two hours of creative effort performed
day after day are sufficient for an intellectual
endeavor that will take a man far.

Finally, insofar as the Gospel is concerned, we
must recognize our inability to understand fully the
teachings of Scripture. Our job is to try to put into
practice those few things which we have truly assim-
ilated and which have taken root in the depths of our
life. After summing up in a few very simple rules
that word of God which has struck us most forcibly,
we must constantly return to it. Thus will we build
the inner man. Bit by bit we will see a unity
establishing itself in our person.

2. *Understanding men as they are*

We must strive for a Christian engagement in the
human society around us. We must discover in our
own field, in our place of work, the means of radi-
ating—perhaps without a word—the presence of
Christ. For you must accept a man where you find
him, how you find him, in order to enter into his

humanity and understand him from within. In such an acceptance it will no longer be a question of judging him but only of loving him with a love that understands everything. The world, which knows little of the Gospel, knows that we profess a fraternal love among all men and on the strength of this often makes astonishing demands upon us. We must remain sensitive to these demands in order to respond to them. The younger generation has a thirst for the authentic. It hates trickery and Christian pharisaism and will not tolerate ready-made solutions. Our Christianity must be rooted in the concrete situations of today's world.

3. *Being weak with the weak and the little ones of this world*

The popular mind readily confuses Christianity and power. We must restore a clearly delineated Christian way of life and refuse vigorously any collusion of spiritual with temporal. If Our Lord by his coming has "exalted the humble and cast down the mighty from their thrones," can we still seek an alliance with the powerful? In addition, we are often enough called to order today by the working class, which is sensitive to any form of power exercised on the part of Christians. The brutal judgment often made against us in this respect is often unjust, but it can serve as a tonic.

There is in man a positive need for self-affirmation which often degenerates into a need for strength and power. The origin of this movement within us remains complex and difficult to analyse, yet this difficulty does not justify a manifestation of human power in the Church.

Must we seek a Christian spirituality of frustration, weakness, and even abjection? Such extremes of faith should be left to the saints. Let us rather have a spirituality of limitation and remind ourselves that it is "when we are weak, then are we strong" in God. We must know our own limits and recognize certain thorns in our own flesh. Yet, in all of this we can never forget that we remain the victorious ones of Christ, destined to live in the joy of the Kingdom.

In this way will we remain closer to the little ones of this world. Theirs is the Kingdom. Happy are the poor.

Living in the Church

Unite so that the world may believe

FUTURE generations will be less and less willing to accept the contradiction of Christians divided into different creeds. They will no longer tolerate the waste of the energies expended in justifying credal standpoints at a time when, because of the staggering growth of populations, the number of men who do not know God grows larger every day. They will no longer put up with a situation in which Christians spend their best efforts proving the solidity of the foundations which support their particular opinions.

The desire for self-justification, contained in germ within every ecclesiastical grouping, has led us to an impasse. At first glance this sickness among Christians seems incurable. It is so powerful that it leads men and women newly converted to an authentic faith in Christ as God and glowing with a fervent love for Christ and their brothers to shut themselves up in their own group within the Church. They come to accept complacent positions of ecclesiastical rigidity once incompatible with the first surging of their faith. The poison of disunity is so insidious that it is not recognized by those affected by it. Once plunged in Christian life with an incomparable zeal, these same Christians can find themselves ten or twenty years later without fire, without love, pre-occupied above all with shielding a so-called spiritual patrimony and animated in this defence by the blind human passions which lead to a spirit of separatism.

How can one hope under such conditions for a universal mission, now more than ever a question of life or death for the Gospel? The Gospel exhorts Christians to win all men. It plants in each the leaven of universality. By shutting us up in Christian ghettos, our divisions have stifled our vitality.

Today, opening our eyes to the scandal of our separation, we seek a visible unity, prerequisite for a missionary drive capable of bringing the Gospel to every man on earth. The universal mission of Christians to unbelievers has everything to gain from such a step. From its very beginnings the Church was characterized by this universal mission, this aware-ness that every man was to be won to the obedience of Jesus Christ. Unity and mission are forever linked.

Only in this way can we constantly make our own the prayer of Christ which is the basis of all ecumen-ism: "That they may be one as we are one . . . that the world may believe that you have sent me . . ."

On the eve of his death Christ foresaw the tragedy
of our divisions. As he was about to leave us he
prayed the more ardently "that they may be one."
By this prayer he sounded the call to unity for Christians of every age. As long as those who profess his
name oppose one another, as long as there is no unity
among them, the world will not be able to believe
that they are sons of the same Father. Hypocrisy, of
old condemned by Christ in the Pharisees, will once
again be introduced into the world, and by Christians
themselves.

"Christ cannot be divided." The body of Christ
is one. All of those who bear the name of Christian
must see to it that their divisions are not an occasion
of scandal for the unbelieving, for the world. Do we
realize that the world has every right to mock us
who, while so glibly confessing a God of love,
nevertheless despise one another even though we all
bear the name of Christ? It is no wonder that our
testimony is rejected when we turn toward the de-
Christianized masses and the pagans of mission
lands.

The new awareness of the existence of the non-
Christian masses and of their hostility toward those
who claim to be of Christ will lead some to discover
the urgent need for our unity. It will open us to an
elementary sense of catholicity. A fresh wind is
blowing among the scattered Christian creeds and a

single question is posing itself more and more: What does it mean to belong to the Church, the Body of Christ? With growing generosity and a true spirit of friendship for all men many among us are rediscovering the universal values implied by Church unity. It is not a question of loving only those who confess Jesus Christ in the same way that I do and who pray in the manner to which I am accustomed. Indeed, if I love only those who love me, what is there in that; do not the pagans do as much?

We must realize that a house divided against itself is in danger of falling. On that day when he comes again, will the Son of Man find faith on the earth? We must be aware of the drama unfolding within and without the Church. If we continue to present a divided front to the world, what answer can we make to a humanity which realizes our inconsistencies better than we do ourselves?

Certain Christians, it is true, claim that the unity of the Church already exists invisibly in Christ. But what is this spiritual unity which is incapable of impressing itself on the facts? Above all, how can we ask that those whom the Gospels call the world, the unbelievers, should see things with the eyes of faith? The world believes in what it sees, and what it sees is a divided Christianity. Only our visible union could prove to the world that we are sons of the same Father, faithful to the same Christ.

If we seek this visible unity of Christians, it is simply out of obedience to the will of Christ expressed in his last prayer: "That they may be one so that the world may believe." Only in this spirit does it become possible to seek the conditions of a true ecumenism, implying purification on both sides in a common love of Jesus Christ.

To lay out the paths of ecumenism it is necessary first of all to close off all sidetracks. They are of different kinds:

1. *Confusionism*

Some Christians prefer to ignore the true causes of division. They believe that it is enough to confess the name of Jesus in order to achieve unity and think that all differences are finally reducible simply to questions of psychology, history, and vocabulary. This is a dangerous route. True ecumenism requires a courageous honesty. Nothing is to be gained by denying the true causes of division, by refusing to define the points of disagreement.

On the other hand, there is a temptation to reject every attempt toward Christian unity by branding it at the outset as confusionism. In such a way the spring of ecumenism is poisoned at its source.

The term confusionism properly applies only to those cases in which the goal is not visible unity but a compromise in invisible unity.

2. *Pragmatism*

Pragmatism consists in attributing all differences to the infernal work of theologians. The pragmatist refuses any attempt to come to an understanding of theological studies and restricts himself to a search for unity on the practical level alone. Within this classification are found all of those social and philanthropic programs which are supposed to unite Christians over and above their differences and which are thought to be in themselves sufficient to do away with the difficulties heaped up by the theologians. In reality any such conception of unity is entirely insufficient, although it remains true that a collaboration in charitable efforts can be a magnificent means of smoothing the way for a total unity in faith.

A common struggle against materialism, a sort of crusade against the world of atheism is also sometimes proposed. Such a rallying of Christians against other men would actually be quite contrary to charity and, in any case, the only testimony to which the world will listen is that of a unity in peace among Christians.

3. *Federalism*

We must also give up the idea of a federation of churches. A federalist structure, often a very happy solution in human societies, has nothing whatever to do with the profound unity of the mystical Body of Christ.

4. *Eschatologism*

In the eschatological position one thinks of unity as a purely invisible thing among different Christian groups. It will appear in its fulness only at the end of time with the coming of Christ. Now, the return of Christ will indeed see the gathering of Christians around the great Shepherd, but we must realize the scandal presented this very day by the visible division of those who confess the same Lord. Even though no one can say with certainty that unity will be realized at this or that point in history—it will be achieved when and how God wishes—nevertheless, ecumenism is a movement raised up by the Holy Spirit to reunite all Christians in a visible way within our own world.

5. *Reunionism*

We are impatient; the Lord knows patience well. We must learn to wait for some things to ripen. It would be unwise to try to force reunions which would not be based on an organically mature unity. Reunionism is the collective form of proselytism. It seeks the immediate return of parts of Christendom to the fold of an ecclesiastical body. Does such an attitude obey the patience of God?

In our unending search for purification we should note well two interior attitudes incompatible with ecumenism:

6. Sectarianism

This spirit may be encountered on every level of human thought. It involves a subtle temptation, a satisfaction with oneself in one's own doctrine. This attitude would have us indulge in a gratifying sense of being superior with the superiority due the truth. We should realize that each of us is in danger of falling into this trap, and especially those of us who have a theological vocation.

7. Integrism

To pass on the whole of the spiritual patrimony of the Church to those who will come after us, to defend the integrity of the faith—who will dare to say that this is not to think and act as a follower of Our Lord?

Yet in the same way that sectarianism, under cover of defending the truth, hardens itself into opposition, so integrism becomes rigid, abrupt, unconditional. One prepares himself for battle—it is no longer a question of truth in charity—in order to defend what he believes to be an unassailable spiritual patrimony. Such an attitude can be found among all Christian groups. The ecumenical movement, by promoting a dialogue among the churches, introduces a new climate. In such a way the Orthodox Church in agreeing to take part in this movement even while preserving its claim to be the only church to possess the whole of the truth has allowed many Protestants to come to appreciate ecclesiastical truths they had previously ignored.

*   *   *

Now let us proceed to a consideration of the principles which should inspire and guide the search for unity among Christians.

1. *The dialogue*

Instead of delivering long monologues in which we hear only our own voice we must learn to listen in order to understand and appreciate from the inside the thought and the position of the man with whom we are speaking. The dialogue demands that we make an effort to break out of our own proper way of thinking according to familiar lines and categories and try to learn how to answer the other man within his own system, thus making him more open. To carry on a dialogue we must give up our polemical arguments and determine to view the other as he wishes to be and not as we are inclined to see him through an image which has come down to us from centuries of sterile opposition. It is a question of striving for a reciprocal contact and a mutual penetration, of learning to appreciate a theology, a philosophy, a spirituality, and sometimes even a scale of moral values so entirely different from our own that often they seem to have no relationship. All of this simply because we must love one another in the truth. This will always require taking the time to find just the right tone, getting rid of our suspicions, revealing ourselves as we are. The dialogue is the opposite of polemic.

Through the centuries we have developed the habit of passing sweeping judgments. It is easy to hand down quick condemnations from the heights which we claim for ourselves as long as they bear only upon other Christians. But true understanding is found only in love. Such an understanding involves not only a thorough familiarity with another's positions but also an attempt to love in him his motives, his reasoning and his conclusions. It demands that we love the position of our neighbor in its development through the history of the Church, that we try to enter into his prayer and his reflection, that we strive to understand the reasons which compel our neighbor to think and to pray differently from us.

2. *Purity of intention*

The attempt at dialogue must conceal no hidden

motives. We are together because God has called us
and not because we are to convert one another. To
launch out on the path of ecumenism with the pre-
conceived intention of converting the other to our
own way of thinking is to betray the ecumenical
spirit at the outset. Only a purity of intention permits an irenic exchange, the first step in great
initiatives within the Church of Jesus Christ. With
full confidence in each other let us carry on a frank
exchange which will deepen our mutual understanding.

3. *Prayer*

Without prayer for unity the work of ecumenism
will be dry and hollow. When we encounter the
difficulties erected by sin and human traditions on
both sides and when our progress is halted by the
deep-seated differences which are constantly emerg-
ing, prayer can revive our hope and love. When we
pray for unity we ask the mercy of the Lord. We
humble ourselves for our faults and for the obstacles which we ourselves place in the way. We
intercede for all of those who work especially for
unity, that in and through God they may become instruments of unity. When at prayer we should also
remain conscious of the full dimensions of the
Church, placing ourselves within the communion of
saints. Finally, in giving thanks we should bear in

mind all that God has already accomplished, he who is the author of such unity. Upon his promises we rest in peace.

4. *Patience*

Our every action, our every prayer should be marked with the patience of God. We know that his ways are not our own. In the search for those ways one of the essential virtues in those engaged in the ecumenical dialogue is patience. It is humanly unthinkable that centuries-old divisions should be bridged immediately. This would require an upheaval that the spirit of man cannot even imagine. God is engaged in the work; we are his workmen. Our part is to continue working and praying with perseverance and fidelity.

5. *Poverty according to the spirit*

Laymen or clergy who have received a call to ecumenism should constantly look to the little ones, the humble among God's people. The clumsy gesture of a poor woman speaks of a fervor which would guard us against rigorism and make us more attentive to the fact that Christian truth is revealed in all of God's people. Each is given his own portion, the charism by which he will add his own nuance to the voice of the Church. Each must listen carefully to the faith which completes his own since it also contributes to the harmony of the great choir of the communion of saints.

With our eyes fixed upon the humble we must recall the prophetic vision in which it was given to the Virgin Mary to announce that the coming of Christ has exalted the lowly and cast down the strong and the mighty. And we ourselves, men of the Church, are we not often among the strong of this world?

Living the Tension
Between Church
and World

CONSIDERING the urgency and scope of the question posed by the presence of the Christian at the heart of the life of the one universal Church and in the center of the life of men, it may seem pretentious to speak in this context of the modest answer emanating from Taizé. We are well aware of the contrast between our very human efforts and the vistas which confront us, horizons so vast that a mere glance at them is disconcerting. It is well to remain modest.

But the Word is made flesh. Witnesses to the Word we must, in the weakness of our humanity, respond as lucidly and as lovingly as possible to the demands which the Word makes upon us. Thus our common service of Jesus Christ resounds to two dominant themes, the search for unity among Christians and the will to be in contact with certain nerve centers of human life. The very equilibrium of our vocation in community is in balance in the tension between these two poles.

It is not without risks and difficulties that one seeks to realize this common life in the Church and in the world. Christians are often fearful when confronted with new experiences, timid, desirous of preserving the conformism of a spiritual patrimony. As for the world, we run the risk of seeking refuge there in hopes of finding a new atmosphere, of breathing more freely than is possible in some aging Christian circles.

The inner call to unity among Christians is constantly renewed within us by our concern to live in conformity with the Gospel. In commanding us to love all men the Gospel does not allow us to continue in an attitude of hostility toward any Christian group. The will to live out the evangelical profession of love conceals an incalculable force, well suited to assist in the eventual overthrow of denominational barriers.

Those who live in such a spirit do not feel called upon to judge the Christians who went before them. They simply believe that, for themselves, an irreversible determination is called for, since they cannot any longer take part in struggles among divided Christian groups. In a sense they have become conscientious objectors in the face of the folly of a divided Christendom.

For our part, we refuse to allow ourselves to be enclosed in a complacent confessional conscience, and are seeking according to our means to open a breach in the barriers which separate Christians. Such a mission requires a continuity from generation to generation and a loving patience. A monastic community is ideally equipped for such a continuity, whatever waves of enthusiasm or doubt may break around it for or against ecumenism.

Without an appreciation of the Churches of today, of their treasures and their deficiencies, without a life of prayer carried on at the very heart of the life of the Church, we could not take up the difficult experiment under which we send forth some of our brothers "on mission" to the crossroads of human life.

In the twenty-one years that separate us from our foundation we have come to realize that the danger of escapism, considered by many of our friends as a part of monastic life, has not in our case been that menacing shadow of a retreat into the safety of the Christian circles—what we call the ghetto—more "cloistered" than any convent. The true danger is quite different and much more subtle. It lies in the attraction of this world, in which we often find among unbelievers more lucidity and self-criticism, a more lively sense of the human, more good will and an unwillingness to pass judgment on others than can be found among some Christians. Such are the values which must flourish among Christians if they would not be condemned to a slow asphyxiation. In the world we have often been able to regain our path simply because we had more room in which to breathe. It is tempting to abandon our older Christian institutions and to install ourselves solely at the nerve centers of human life.

Thus it can be dangerous to send young brothers forth into the world of the working class. There they find in unionism a thirst for justice and a desire for practical solutions which is too often lacking in Christian circles, even though they know from the Beatitudes the desire for justice among men. Before building the tower, then, we must sit down and examine our capacities, the material needed for the construction. Not everyone can run the risk of this adventure, but some people must. They have received the gifts; they must make use of them. Christians enter the struggle with the force promised them by the Lord of the Church and of the universe. Are they to be the only ones to allow themselves to be stopped because they fear the dangers and temptations of the world?

The aim of our calling is the service in common of Jesus Christ. Service in common, however, does not necessarily require that we be united under one roof, but rather that the community remain well coordinated despite its dispersion throughout the world. We desire to serve boldly, we wish to go where other Christians cannot go because of legitimate responsibilities. We want to take up positions in outposts at the nerve centers of human life.

Our vocation has taught us how to find a balance in a life situated at the intersection between Church and world.

We have before us two types of service—contemplation and action. They do not by any means exclude each other, and we have tried to unite them. Had our calling been purely contemplative, we would have concentrated solely on objective prayer, the prayer of the Church in all of the centuries of the past, without the necessity of making contact with the men of today. Because we were called also to a life in the midst of men we have oriented our interior life toward what we call, clumsily perhaps, an "athletic" spirituality, incarnating the human in the whole of our Christian existence, doing battle in the spirit St. Paul points out to us: "I chastise my body so as to bring it into subjection, lest having preached to others I myself become a castaway."

If there is a spirituality of Taizé it consists in nothing other than the desire to "run" according to the counsel of St. Paul. To run together and no longer alone, this means abandoning a search for a purely individual salvation in order to seek the sal-

vation of all. This course leads us on toward the
finish line; we can run only if together we fix our
eyes on the Christ of glory.

The strength necessary for this common training
we draw from the treasury of prayer of all centuries
which unites us morning, noon, and night and has
formed our common life. This same prayer sends
us forth into the world to witness to the joy and love
of Christ.

To help us to remain faithful in this service of
God there have been given us three great signs which
constantly recall to us the absolute character of our
vocation. By them we belong to the great family of
monasticism. It would be well to turn to them now
so as to understand them more fully.

Celibacy

THE chastity of celibacy is possible only because of Christ and the Gospel. Those who have abandoned wife, children, fields . . . do well to keep this in mind. If a man refuses this vision he is condemned in advance to bitterness, failure and perhaps spiritual decay. The fulness of Christian life, as great in celibacy as in marriage, is destroyed at its base.

This reality is so difficult to grasp that we cannot condemn those who do not understand the teaching of Christ on celibacy. He said himself: "He alone can understand to whom it has been given."

This must be underlined: the teaching of Christ on marriage and on celibacy remains as revolutionary today as the first day it was pronounced. To realize this it is necessary only to place one's self once again in the climate of the Ancient Covenant.

Marriage was held in Israel to be a natural obligation, signed always by the "increase and multiply."

It was necessary above all to insure descendants to Abraham; thus the insistence on procreation with a view toward the survival of the people of Israel. But if we remember the ease with which one could obtain a divorce—was not a simple letter of divorce sufficient to break conjugal ties?—we realize that monogamy in Israel risked being polygamy through successive monogamies. In this way one preserved the primitive commandment, "Thou shalt not commit adultery," while at the same time salving his moral conscience.

Since by religious law everyone was bound to marry, we can say that at the moment of the coming of Christ in Israel the vocation to marriage did not really exist, since there was no freely-consented choice.

Christ came to establish a new order. Henceforth there were to be in the Church two vocations confronting each man, both difficult, filled with renunciations, limitations and sacrifices. Truly monogamous marriage, from which all possibility of divorce is excluded, is no more natural to the heart of fallen man than celibacy. From this point forward it was no longer necessary to insure at all costs a posterity to Abraham. Jesus himself, truly man and truly God, accepted for himself the choice of celibacy for the sake of the Kingdom of Heaven.

Marriage and celibacy are both Christian absolutes; because of Christ both of them become signs of the approaching kingdom. Both impose hardships in life which cannot be borne except for love of Christ and the Gospel.

The Reform, concerned though it has always been with Scriptural foundations, has often returned, as far as celibacy is concerned, to an Old Testament position. The sixteenth century was more aware of certain abuses of ecclesiastical celibacy than concerned with its scriptural value. Without a doubt a lack of theology concerning celibacy has led to a refusal on the part of the general run of Protestants to accept an engagement in Christian celibacy. Most people rebel when faced with the renunciation of the love of a man for a woman.

How can we expect this tension to disappear as long as we refuse to recognize Christian celibacy as a call of God? At most we are willing to accept the practical utility of celibacy, applying to it the words of St. Paul. Yet the true vocation of celibacy is the extreme sign of contradiction which it represents in the midst of a hardened world, which has ears but does not hear, which needs visible signs. In the sexualized climate of the western world, a life offered in authentic chastity in the name of Christ poses a startling question.

Why this renunciation? It is a matter of obedience to a scriptural scale of values which is not that of

nature. The vocation of celibacy takes on its true
worth when it is incarnated in men and women,
creatures of flesh and blood, sometimes fiery spirits,
passionate and rich in human capacities and sensibilities. The monastic vocation, this sign of contradiction, can be responded to anywhere, by men or
women in a factory, on the farm, or in learned circles.

Here we must again insist that both Christian
marriage and Christian celibacy are valid only in
terms of an effort at obedience to the Lord of the
Church, with the sole aim of loving him more. They
will never narrow a man if undertaken for the love
of Christ and neighbor. Approached in any other
spirit, they will quickly become merely a return to
preoccupation with one's self in which we no longer
love for the sake of Christ and the Gospel, and in
which our love, far from giving of itself, will seek
above all to possess and dominate everything for its
own satisfaction. In such a way, because they seek
only a natural happiness, the best of couples can
make their home a prison dedicated to death. Christian parents can reach a point at which they love
their children only for their own satisfaction. Do
not certain celibates also fall into this trap? Their
exaggerated sensibilities and fear of frankness stifle
them in an introverted self-consciousness and make
them hypersensitive.

If the love of Christ does not seize our being in its

totality, if we do not allow ourselves to be enkindled by his love, we cannot aspire to the fulness of Christian marriage or of Christian celibacy.

For all those who have entered the great family of monasticism, the final commitment to celibacy manifests their desire to become men of a single love. The monastic vocation—as is clear from the original meaning of the word, a call to solitude—implies for the man who accepts it a certain solitude with God. Committed to a true love of the unseen God without hating the men whom he sees, the man who lives such a calling feeds his capacity for love at the unique source, Christ himself. Through the chastity of celibacy he tends to become a man of a single love.

One question remains. How can we presume to bind ourselves for life if the demands of marriage are so great? This is almost exactly the question of the disciples. As to celibacy, we have asked ourselves whether we have the right to bind ourselves for life. Is this not to limit the freedom of the Holy Spirit? But in such reasoning are we not posing restrictions on the freedom of God merely to keep from committing ourselves, as though God were not free and powerful enough to make known his call?

For ourselves there was but one answer—to commit ourselves entirely on the strength of the promises of Christ: "He who leaves father, mother, wife, children . . . will receive a hundredfold in this world and life everlasting in the next." The moment we make a covenant with Christ, He joins Himself to us. Experience has borne out this truth and has confirmed in us a vocation which can perhaps be fully understood only by those to whom it has been given.

If celibacy brings greater availability to concern oneself with the things of God, it is acceptable only in order to give oneself more fully to one's neighbor with the very love of Christ.

Our celibacy means neither breaking with human affections, nor indifference, but calls for the transformation of our natural love. Only Christ converts the passions into total love for one's neighbor. When the selfishness of the passions is not surpassed by growing generosity, when your heart is not constantly filled with an immense love, you can no longer let Christ love within you and your celibacy will become a burden.

This work of Christ within you demands infinite patience.

(The Rule of Taizé)

The commitment to chastity is a call to live a radical purity, and this under conditions of life which are sometimes hazardous. It is no exaggeration to speak of an heroic chastity, engaged in a necessary struggle which binds us body and soul to Christ.

Through purity of heart we come to see God. "Blessed are the pure of heart, for they shall see God." We must rest upon this promise of seeing God—of seeing him soon, of seeing him already in our earthly life. Finally, this alone will be important. Without this desire to see Christ we cannot hope to persevere in purity of heart and flesh. Without this expectation, kept alive and renewed within us by the silent contemplation of the very person of Christ the Lord, all purity is unthinkable. To such an extent does the final and irreversible rejection of all carnal desires, even in imagination, seem destined to produce a blind rebellion, so great is the need which cries out in every being for satisfaction, and, it must be admitted, for a satisfaction through physical intimacy.

To remain chaste, to answer the call to purity of heart and to live it authentically—only the desire to see Christ will be able to quench this thirst within us. Little by little the things which trouble us, even those whose existence we refuse to acknowledge, will be calmed in spite of themselves by the contemplation of the living Christ in the Gospels and the Christ of glory in the prayer of the Church.

"Pluck out the eye, cut off the hand that scandalize thee." "Do violence to your body." All discipline

can be accepted only for the sake of Christ and the
Gospel. Certainly we must run as good athletes in
the arena, in order to win the prize. Pluck out the
eye in order to form new habits and to bring under
control a whole inner mechanism capable in some
situations of touching off a whole train of imagination. At the end of this path we will find the peace
of our carnal life, with Christ in God.

We must never forget that no attempt at purifying
ourselves to see God can succeed without contemplation. Without this, asceticism betrays itself, pur-
sues an unattainable purity and falls in love with
virtue for its own sake as a seeking of the self.

Only the gaze we keep fixed upon Christ permits
the slow transformation. Little by little natural love
becomes living charity. The change is achieved.
Heart, emotions, senses, human nature—all are still
very much alive, but Another than self transfigures
them.

The Community of
Goods

HOLDING goods in common does not at all exclude the possibility of poverty:

Incalculable strength is given by boldness to make the best use of all present-day goods and to lay up no capital without fear of possible poverty. But if, like the children of Israel, you store up for the morrow the bread which comes from heaven, if you work out projects for the future, you risk overtaxing the Brothers whose vocation it is to live in the immediate present.

(The Rule of Taizé)

In our vocation we run the risk of idealizing poverty. The Gospel never canonized poverty. For Christ, the poor man is the humble man among his people, or the man who does not use his riches to

105

try to possess the soul of his neighbor. Christ lived himself and traced out a path for men. He lived among sinners and understood their humanity. He changed water into wine at Cana to give them joy. He loved the unhappy and stood up against the hardened rich. For does not the earth which the rich have divided among themselves "belong to the Lord, and the fulness thereof?"

A fully accepted poverty can help build a Christian life and render easy a detachment which the possession of goods might hinder. Yet poverty in itself is not the ideal for a Christian:

Poverty has no virtue in itself. The poor according to the Gospel learn to live without the assurance of the morrow, in joyous confidence that they will lack for nothing. The spirit of poverty does not consist in making oneself look poor, but in setting everything in the simple beauty of creation. The spirit of poverty is to live in the gladness of today. If God gives gratuitously the good things of the earth, it is blessed for man to give that which he has received.

(The Rule of Taizé)

In every Christian life money plays a basic role. It can as easily be a Satanic force as a means to spiritual activity. Not everyone is capable of using possessions as though he used them not, remaining open to the possibility of poverty if one day that be called for.

Why do we wear ourselves out in feverish activities? We are ruled in spite of ourselves by a shame in being poor. For poverty is looked down upon. The worldly prejudice teaches that a certain income corresponds to a certain level of education. By "education" is understood certain external customs and artificial habits, the whole complex of needs which rules us without our even being aware of our bondage. Yet if this very night your soul be demanded of you, who will profit from the goods you have accumulated?

Those who profess the common life are not thereby exempt from concern for their daily bread, above all if they live solely by means of their labor. They know that there is a long way between the teaching "sufficient to the day is the evil thereof" and its application.

Possessing goods in common takes on its true value only if we live in the boldness of God— bearing all hardships together, living if necessary in the most miserable of dwellings, and, if no resources are available, persevering in our mission despite poverty.

We must dare to live precariously, setting out like Abraham, who did not know where he was going. We must know how to abandon ourselves in the confidence that from day to day our needs will be provided for. In this way we will keep far from us the spirit of possessiveness.

If our common ownership of property applied only to material goods, it would be limited indeed. It must lead us to a community of spiritual goods, both sorrows and joys.

Recognize your mistakes with simplicity, in the transparency of brotherly love, without finding therein a pretext for discerning those of the others. Wherever they are, the Brothers practice brief and frequent sharing of their concerns with each other.

(The Rule of Taizé)

The transparency of one man toward another does not imply pouring out confidences about oneself, but rather an openness of the whole person. It would be a mistake to confuse confiding in a brother with confession. Confession is made to the Lord of heaven and earth in the presence of a man who has received such a ministry.

There were periods in the Church when poverty presented a sign of contradiction capable of inspiring peoples who were barely Christianized. Today, with no fear of personal poverty, Christians must be careful to manifest the dedication of their lives by the will to distribute among all men the riches accumulated in some areas of the globe. A great challenge has been given the Church by a doctrine which, atheistic in its premises, fights for the redistribution of wealth.

Christians today are struck with blindness and hardness of heart when they can no longer grasp the primitive evangelical vocation of Christians who "held all things in common." They forget or ignore the fact that, throughout the first centuries of the Church, this preoccupation dominated the works of the great doctors of the Church, so clearly did they sense the danger of compromise. It is for us to meditate peacefully on their teachings. These teachings are sufficient in themselves. But first of all let us pose a question: Could not the Church, ever the light shining in the darkness, rejoice if the principles of community were transferred to the world and became, instead of evangelical precepts, human laws? This would not necessarily mean that the world had become Christian. Under the influence of the Gospel the world would have advanced to a temporal order which the Church could always consider a lesser evil.

We must listen to St. Ambrose of Milan: "It was in common and for all, rich and poor, that the earth was created. Why then, O rich, do you claim for yourselves a monopoly on owning land? Nature knows no rich, it gives birth only to poor infants. . . . It is not from your riches that you give alms to the poor, it is a bit of what is already theirs that you give back, for it is a common good given for all that you usurp for yourselves. The earth belongs to all, not only to the rich."

St. John Chrysostom is no less definite: "It is because some try to have for themselves that which belongs to all that quarrels and wars break out, as though nature were angered with man, who with the cold phrase 'mine and thine' raises discord where God has put unity. . . . These words 'mine and thine' are empty of sense and expressive of no reality whatever. Those are the goods of the poor, of which you are custodians, even though you possess them from honest labor or by inheritance. . . . The greatest injury which riches do to you is that they separate you from the blessed servitude of Jesus Christ."

Basil of Caesarea continues in the same tone: "But these goods are mine, do I not have the right to keep them? What do you mean by 'yours'? From where did you get this right? From where did you bring it into the world? It is as though someone grabbed a place in a theater and then tried to keep all others from entering and enjoyed it all by himself, as if he had an exclusive right to a spectacle destined for a community. Such are the rich. They consider common goods as belonging to them because they got them first. . . . If you call a house your 'own,' you have said nothing. In fact the air and the earth and every dwelling place belong to the Creator (just as do you yourselves who have built them) and everything without exception. . . . The community of goods is a more adequate mode of existence than private property, and the only one which conforms to nature."

Again, Chrysostom says: "Is it not an evil to keep for one's self that which belongs to the Lord, to enjoy alone a good which is everyone's? And the earth, is it not God's, and all that earth contains? If our riches belong to the Lord of the world, they also belong to all men, who are his servants like ourselves, because all that belongs to the Lord is for the use of all."

Accepting an Authority

THE principle of authority in a community corresponds to a practical need for unity:

There is no hope of a bold and total service of Jesus Christ without unity of mind. Individualism disintegrates the Community and halts its advance.

(The Rule of Taizé)

Certainly the ideal would be to take no decision that is not a unanimous one. But idealism is not a biblical notion. If we waited for unanimity before moving, the community would very soon become static. This is a fact of life: one must always advance; he who tries to stand still will actually be slipping backwards.

Would majority rule on all decisions which affect the community be the best procedure? Doubtfully so, for it would mean the imposition of a method of

human society onto the Church. The will of the
Lord would have to express itself by fifty-one per-
cent of the votes. In a community, such a method
would almost immediately give rise to intrigues and
politics.

Within the Church, to take a decision is to follow
in the footprints of God and to commit all Christians to a practical path of service. Authority in a
community can only be Christocentric. He who has
received this responsibility must first scrutinize the
designs of God and then take the practical decision.
It goes without saying that all have a share in this
search. The Council, in which all professed members
take part:

seeks all the light possible concerning the will of
Christ for the advance of the Community. The first
step is therefore to establish silence in oneself so as
to prepare to listen to one's Lord. Nothing is more
contrary to the spirit of the Council than search
which is not purified by the sole desire to discern
God's will. The Council is above all the occasion
when it is incumbent upon you to seek peace and
pursue it, to eschew contention, and the temptation
to be proved right. Avoid a tone that brooks no
reply, the categorical 'we must.' Do not build up
good arguments in order to make yourself heard;
explain in a few words what seems to you to conform

most closely to God's plan, without imagining that you may be able to impose it. To avoid one seeking to outdo another in argument, the Prior is responsible before his Lord for making the decisions without being bound by a majority. Freed from human pressures, he listens to the most timid Brother with the same attention he gives to the Brother who is full of self-assurance. If the Prior senses a lack of profound agreement on an important question, let him reserve judgment, and, in order to go forward, make a provisional decision, ready to return to it later; for immobility is disobedience for Brothers advancing toward Christ.

(The Rule of Taizé)

The task of the Prior is thus to lead on toward Christ. He must see to it that all possible continuity in the march of the community toward Christ is maintained and must protect the community from internal divisions, for the sower of discord is always there seeking critical situations in order to separate what should be united. Here also let us have no false spiritualism. If the unity is not visible, if it does not strike the eye, we can no longer speak of spiritual unity.

As soon as we speak of the charge given a man in the field of Church government we must also bear in mind his grave responsibilities:

Making decisions is a formidable charge for the Prior. In this guidance of souls let him be watchful not to create subservience, but to build up the whole body in Christ. Let him seek the particular gifts of each Brother, so that the Brother may be led to discover them. Let him not consider his charge as being superior, nor yet assume it with false humility, remembering only that it has been entrusted to him by Christ, to whom he will have to render account for this charge. Let him break any authoritarianism within himself, but have no weakness in maintaining his Brothers in the design of God. Let him prevent those of an authoritarian disposition from dominating, and let him show confidence to the weak. Let him arm himself with mercy, asking Christ to grant it as the grace most essential to him.

(The Rule of Taizé)

But by what right does a man speak up in the community? By the authority of the Word of God. The Lord of the Church causes his Word to be heard through the mouths of men. He gives the necessary gifts, including the discernment of spirits. In themselves human words have no authority. They receive it only from God.

He is thus in an infinitely perilous situation who must proclaim the Word of God. Often he would prefer to refuse his Lord, who obliges him to speak

with full authority. The sins of the man, will they
not become mixed with his words? This is a serious
question, one which demands a constant vigilance.
He who exercises it knows that authority is true only
in the spirit of prayer. It demands that he deny
himself in order to search, together with those in his
charge, the sovereign will. How can a man exhort
and rebuke without being himself a living sermon
on self-forgetfulness? Misunderstandings, bitter dis-
appointments, betrayals of all kinds—these are the
crosses which must be born patiently by a man who
holds authority in the Church, with a full acceptance
of this school of humiliation.

Unless we forget ourselves, how shall we be able
to judge objectively? Our sensitivity and self-love,
which are constantly being wounded, must be buried
in order to give full place to the judgment of God.
Then true authority is given to the human word in
the community, in the attempt to bring together that
which is separated. If one day authority shows itself
firm, if it is forced to have recourse to law, this will
never be simply to make its own task easier but will
always be done in the sorrow of being otherwise
unable to make clear the sovereign will to a man who
refuses to submit himself to grace.

Authority has nothing to do with human con-
straint or with the imposition of one's own will. It
can never substitute itself for any man's conscience;

its role is to recall the will of Christ. He who bears this responsibility must ever guard against the secret ambition which inclines one unwittingly to the will to dominate souls and to appropriate them for oneself—ambition infinitely more perilous than that of the princes of this earth, who rule over men's possessions and their bodies. His role is to decrease so that Christ may increase in those entrusted to him.

Allowing Christ to Kindle in Us the Fire of His Love

IF we are to remain ardent in God's present day, the living charity of Christ must come and fan the flame within us and renew our friendship for our neighbor, our brother.

Paradoxical though it may be, we know that it is often easier to live with a man who does not know God than with a Christian. In the midst of the life of the world we can, without stirring up all sorts of defense mechanisms, try to insure a presence of Christ and to be leaven in the dough. How much more difficult is friendship among Christians. The age of the Christian societies and their division into various denominations strain their relations to the point of rendering such a friendship precarious. We risk being bogged down in a terrain cluttered through the centuries with emotional elements. Our reasoning power is vitiated. It becomes incapable of performing its true function, the search for truth in charity.

If there can be no question of diluting the truth, we must insist nevertheless that there is no truth without charity. Today the first demand of charity in dealings among Christians requires that we reject the attitude, so easy and so attractive to the natural man, which consists in setting oneself up as judge. Without a conversion to the love of Jesus Christ we cannot hope for a thorough transformation of our credal positions, forged as they have been through so many generations of Christians.

A stage in our progress toward unity will consist in gaining this firm hope, that the Lord will lead us to unity. He has the power to do so. Our part is not to offer any objections to the means he chooses.

Already beginning to arise in the depths of many consciences is the question: Must we hope for unity at any price? Yes, because such was the final will of Christ: "That all may be one . . . that the world may believe." Visible unity is not just one human aspiration among many but a positive command of faith. It is not motivated by any external circumstance of our world; it is obedience to Christ.

The inner attitude which will permit this new obedience has its source in a life in Christ. Such a life arouses in us not a sentimental nostalgia for unity but a manly strength to bring crashing down upon themselves the divisions which fragment so much of our vital energy.

We must love the Church as Christ has loved her, and accept the fact that her only path lies across deep ruts dug by the sins of her children in their spirit of division and complacency. We must love her despite the mediocrity of some of those who hold heavy responsibilities within her. We must love the Church in her members—in the best of her children, but also in those who are most thoroughly compromised.

In such a way does the Church of Christ proceed through the ages. She is alive to the degree that her institutions are animated by the charity of the faithful. She is strong when her members arm themselves day after day with the infinite patience of the faith. She is humble when her children, far from judging her with the harshness of complacency, love her enough to give their lives in the attempt to renew her institutions this day and every day.

Any other path leads only to a spirit of self-sufficiency and to schisms which do nothing to amend the faults of the condemned institutions.

Judgments from without can only harden and close in on themselves those who feel that they are being judged. We cannot help recognizing the fact that neither the firm stand nor the just reasonings of the Reformers who left their denomination led to the reform of a Church whose transformation they called for with such hope. There is no question of underestimating the necessity of their cry. It was unavoidable. But after their day there was no hope for reform as long as the requests on the part of the new Christian groups, themselves so quickly weighed down with a heavy heritage of controversies, were emptied of all love for the reality hidden even in an encrusted tradition.

Only when we empty our hearts of all bitterness and allow ourselves to be filled with an infinite respect for our neighbor will he be able to accept observations and advice. As love of the living Christ increases within us we will no longer want to make our neighbor suffer from a bad conscience. We will learn to love even those who are opposed to one another. Then the Christian walks on solid ground, certain of being in God.

History tells of a man who bore witness to a true reform, St. Francis of Assisi. He suffered for the Church and loved her after the example of Christ. He could have judged the institutions, the customs, the hardness of certain Christians of his own day. But this he refused to do. He preferred to die to himself. He waited with an ardent patience and the day came on which his expectation, burning with charity, was fulfilled in many a renewal of Christian life in the world.

Only Christ can kindle in us today the fire of his love and lead us to a willingness to understand from within a Church alienated from us by four centuries of separation. We shall learn to accept the power of God directing this Church. He has allowed some of its institutions, which had become decayed or had even grown to be a source of scandal, to lapse. One outcome, for example, is that ecclesiastical submission to temporal power no longer exists.

The Lord who led his people out of the desert has the patience to lead them still in sovereign fashion. He knows how to raise up this or that prophet in the midst of his people.

It is demanded of us that we be leaven in the dough. Some of us are asked to express unity by word. Others receive the gift of most fervent intercession. Still others are asked to offer their lives in a giving of themselves which may cost a hard struggle, an oblation whose meaning remains hidden. Through such diverse gifts each Christian must be a ferment of unity in the Church.

The means provided seem small enough indeed. The leaven is so much like the dough that the eye sees no difference. Yet it contains invisibly a perfect efficacy. Within it, all is already contained; by it infinite possibilities become realities.

The leaven is hidden in the dough. Each of us is to stand at the heart of the life of the Church and the life of men by means of a discreet presence, as in the case of every life hidden with Christ in God.

And that which we renew will perhaps harden in its turn, as the crust of a pie hardens with the passage of time. We must train others to introduce a new leaven after we are gone. In this way there are renewed in the holy Church of Christ both its institutions and those who animate them.

May our lives be offered in this diversity, and from our poor efforts may there arise, without our knowing how, incalculable consequences.

The day will come, the Apostle tells us, when the gift of tongues and of prophecies will be abolished and knowledge will disappear; but charity will never pass away. Though we should accomplish heroic things, have the fullness of faith, a faith that moves mountains, though we should give what we have as food for the poor, though we go so far as to deliver our bodies to be burned, if we do not have love it will profit us nothing.

We can accomplish wonderful works, but only those will count which proceed from the merciful love of Christ within us. At the end of our lives we will be judged according to love, the love which we have allowed to grow little by little and to spread itself out in compassion for every man living in the Church and in the world.